About the Autho

Stanley B. Kimball

Professor Stanley B. Kimball holds a Ph.D. in Eas┗ Columbia University. He has been at Southern Illinois University at Edwardsville since 1959 and has been traveling the Mormon Trail since 1964. Past President of the Mormon History Association, he is the Historian of the Mormon Trails Association and a trails advisor to the National Park Service offices in Salt Lake City and Santa Fe.

The author of numerous papers, books and articles on Mormon and Western American History, Professor Kimball received the "Best Book Award" from the Mormon History Association in 1981 for the biography of his ancestor, Heber C. Kimball. He has also served as a Trail Guide for *National Geographic,* the *Deseret News* and Sons of Utah Pioneers. Having appeared in three documentary films about the Mormon Trail, Professor Kimball's most recent contribution will be aired in 1997 on PBS in "A Trail of Hope."

A native of Farmington, Utah, and a veteran of World War II, Professor Kimball is married to Violet Tew. They have four children. Professor Kimball observes, "I always had a habit of studying local Mormon history wherever I went."

After moving to Illinois, he began visiting Nauvoo and Carthage, 150 miles north of his home in Edwardsville. "This led to following the Mormon Trail west from Nauvoo and thus it all began more than 30 years ago."

Acknowledgment

The Trail Guide is provided for modern-day travelers who are making their own rediscovery of the Mormon Pioneer Trail and the wagon trains and handcart companies that journeyed along it.

The idea of putting the guide together arose in conversations with Mike Duwe, at that time the National Park Service's Mormon Pioneer Trail Coordinator, and with Stanley B. Kimball. Stan's expertise and research talents are unsurpassed when it comes to the Mormon Pioneer Trail.

Planning, reviewing, proofing and the financing program were rendered by the members of the Trail Guide Committee. In addition to the project director, the committee members include Ronald W. Andersen, Paul Badger, Gar Elison, Jane J. Evert, Dr. Joseph L. Hatch, M. Dell Madsen, Paul Madsen and Richard H. Nebeker.

The fund development program was organized by committee treasurer Gar Elison. Significant financial support was given by the National Park Service, the Utah Crossroads Chapter of the Oregon-California Trails Association, the Salt Lake City Chapter of Sons of Utah Pioneers, the Mormon Trails Association, Intermountain Realty and by individuals.

The proofing and reviewing of the guide was assisted by committee members Ronald W. Andersen, Gar Elison and especially, M. Dell Madsen. Also providing review were Jere Krakow, Superintendent of the National Park Service Long Distance Trails Office, and Kay Threlkeld, Interpretive Planner in the same office. Prefatory material was edited by writer and editor Will Bagley of Salt Lake City and Warren Hatch of Oxford, England.

With the approach of the Trail's sesquicentennial, new trail site markers have been placed. Supplying information on these and other matters were: Karla Gunzenhauser and Bob Brown of the Iowa Mormon Trails Association, Gail Holmes of the Nebraska Mormon Trails Association, Jude Carino of the Wyoming Bureau of Land Management, John Knudson of Utah Division of Parks and Recreation, and the Long Distance Trails Office of the National Park Service in Salt Lake City.

Garn Hatch

Part One
Introduction

C.C.A. Christensen – *The Nauvoo Temple*

America is in the midst of a great western trails renaissance. Our historic trails are now becoming better known, more fully appreciated, more carefully preserved, and more clearly marked. In an effort to preserve the country's historic and recreational resources, Congress enacted the National Trails System Act in 1968. Trails have been added to the system over the years, and there are now 20 national historic and scenic trails, including the Mormon Pioneer National Historic Trail.

The Mormons from the 1840s through the 1860s were very much a part of the great westward surge. This began in the 1820s when fur trappers started exploring the West, searching out mountain passes and vital water sources, and continued through the westering activities of traders, missionaries, and land-hungry settlers, to the completion of the transcontinental railroad in 1869. The Mormons were part of the idea and the realization of the doctrine of Manifest Destiny and the Great Reconnaissance of the West.

Interest in the Mormon Trail has never been greater than it is today. An increasing number of county, state, and

Gary Kapp – *Sunflowers and Buffalo Chips*

federal road signs are being installed to point out historic sites and markers along the trail. This renewal of interest is also evident in the increasing availability of brochures, guides, and printed materials, as well as in the growing number of markers, parks, schools, businesses, museums, exhibits, events, and tourist attractions that pertain to and celebrate the Mormon Trail.

The growing fascination with the Mormon Trail is well deserved. As our national trail heritage gives way to development and urban sprawl, there seems to be a direct relationship between the rapidity with which we destroy this legacy and our desire to write and read about it—even to go in search of it, to experience the power of place and the spirit of locale.

The officially designated Mormon Pioneer National Historic Trail is confined to the route of the Pioneer Party which started February 4, 1846, in Nauvoo, Illinois, and ended 1,300 miles later in present Salt Lake City, Utah, on July 24, 1847. However, the trail was used extensively by some 70,000 Mormons and many other westering people until the completion of the transcontinental railroad in 1869.

This basic trail guide has been prepared for the general traveler who would like to conveniently visit the main historic sites along the pioneer route of 1846-47 in ordinary passenger cars. To that end, this guide provides information regarding the significance of 76 historic sites scattered along the trail and instructions on how to visit them. Sites generally excluded are those which are; particularly difficult to find, located on private land, of minimal importance, four wheel-drive-recommended, not on all-weather roads, or require special maps. An exhaustive guide would detail several hundred known sites and markers, including more than 125 camp sites. Such a definitive guide, however, is clearly beyond the scope of this basic guide and the need of the general traveler.

Since new markers, exhibits, and roadside pullouts are continually being added along the trail, travelers are advised to watch for and visit them. When visiting a site on private land you must obtain the land owner's permission before entering. Since the Mormon Pioneer National Historic Trail is identical with parts of the Oregon, California, and Pony Express trails, travelers should also watch for these related markers en route.

The guide is organized by state—Iowa, Nebraska, Wyoming, and Utah—and proceeds east to west. (One site in Illinois is mentioned.) Every effort has been made to enable the traveler to find the historic sites with the use of ordinary state road maps and the Mormon Pioneer National Historic Trail folder, published by the National Park Service. Occasionally, when such maps do not suffice, insert maps will be provided, or the traveler will be advised to "follow marked roads." At times the traveler will be well advised to "ask locally for directions."

The 1,300-mile-long trek must be divided into two parts—the approximately 265-mile-long section across Iowa in 1846 and the 1,032-mile-long segment across Nebraska and Wyoming and into Utah in l847. The Iowa portion of the trail was used relatively little, mainly by the Mormons fleeing Illinois in l846 and by other Mormons "jumping off" from Keokuk, Iowa, in l853. Part of it was also used in 1856-57 by seven companies of Mormon handcarters from Iowa City, who intersected the 1846 Mormon Pioneer Trail near present Lewis, in Cass County, Iowa.

Many people have contributed much to making this brief guide as accurate and up to date as possible. (Travelers are advised, however, that road numbers and names are changed occasionally with little or no advance notification.)

I wish to thank friends in the Iowa Mormon Trails Association, the Nebraska Mormon Trails Association, the Mormon Trails Association, the Bureau of Land Management, the Oregon-California Trails Association, the Utah Division of Parks and Recreation, and the National Park Service. Special thanks must go to Garn Hatch of the Mormon Trails Association and to Kay Threlkeld and Jere Krakow of the National Park Service Long Distance Trails Office.

Barna Meeker – *Independence Rock*

Part Two

Overview of the Trail

Unknown Artist – *Circling of Wagons*

ACROSS IOWA IN 1846

The Pioneers of 1846 generally followed primitive territorial roads across the monotonous, undifferentiated, rolling central lowlands of Iowa as far as Bloomfield, Davis County. Beyond this point, the trail followed little used Indian and trading trails along ridges from one water source to another until it arrived at an Indian agent's settlement on the Missouri River at present Council Bluffs. The trail always remained within 50 miles of the present Missouri state line. There is very little of the old trail left in Iowa. Time and the plow have erased almost all trail remnants.

On February 4, 1846, the first wagons of the vanguard pulled out of Nauvoo, Illinois, and crossed the Mississippi River on ferries near the present Exodus to Greatness marker in Nauvoo. After crossing the Mississippi, the Pioneers traveled west some 7 miles to a staging ground at Sugar Creek, Lee County, Iowa, to await the arrival of Mormon leader Brigham Young and other church leaders, who joined them February 15.

By March 1 the first group of Mormons were ready to vacate their staging ground. No accurate record was kept of how many wagons and people were assembled at Sugar Creek on that memorable day, but 500 wagons and 3,000 people is probably close.

What from the start was known as the Camp of Israel began to lumber out from Sugar Creek about noon to the "gee-haws" of teamsters and the yells of herdsmen and children. Thereafter, Old Testament parallels to a Zion, a Chosen People, an Exodus, a Mount Pisgah, a Jordan River, a Dead Sea, to being "in the tops of the mountains," and to making the desert blossom like the rose were noted, devised, cherished, and handed down to succeeding generations of Mormons.

A few trail journals give a romantic cast to the exodus across Iowa, that "Mormon Mesopotamia" between the Mississippi and the Missouri Rivers. However, as most other trail accounts make clear, the worst part of the entire journey from Nauvoo to the Valley of the Great Salt Lake was the beginning. Often, when roads did exist, they were most primitive. Although the Mormons made some improvements along the roads and trails they followed across Iowa, they did little, if any, trailblazing.

Along the Iowa trail the basic skills of emigrating and colonizing were practiced, and semipermanent camps were established. This part of the westward march influenced Mormon history long afterward.

As the camp moved west, some changes and improvements in organization became necessary. Only the fundamental arrangement of the trek had been effected at Nauvoo and Sugar Creek.

On March 22 on the Chariton River, near present Sedan, Appanoose County, the emigrants were regrouped into three companies, each with a hundred families. Each company was then subdivided into groups of fifties and then tens, each company led by a captain. The Pioneers remained here March 22-31.

Thereafter, the line of march continued somewhat to the southwest until the companies found themselves on Locust Creek. It was here on April 15 that William Clayton, the Camp Clerk, wrote the words of the now-famous hymn "Come, Come, Ye Saints," often called, with some justification, the "Mormon Marseillaise" or the "Hymn Heard Around the World."

From Locust Creek, the camp bore to the northwest. By April 24 the Pioneers had reached a place which they named Garden Grove. It was located about halfway across Iowa, 145 miles west of Nauvoo and 120 miles east of Council Bluffs. Here, on the east bank of the Weldon Fork of the Grand River, they established the first of several semipermanent camps between Nauvoo and the Missouri River. A town by the name of Garden Grove is now located near this old campsite, and the local school district is named the Mormon Trail District.

Six days and about 35 miles later they established another semipermanent camp and resting place. This site, on the middle fork (Twelve-Mile Creek) of the Grand River and on Pottawattamie Indian land, was named Mount Pisgah after the biblical Pisgah (Deuteronomy 3:27) where Moses viewed the Promised Land.

C.C.A. Christensen – *Winter Quarters*

Late on June 2 the camp moved on toward Council Bluffs, some 90 miles to the west, leaving behind enough people to improve and maintain Mount Pisgah for the benefit of future Mormon emigrants going west. On June 14 the camp reached the Council Bluffs area on the Missouri River, and the first portion of the march was nearly over. The vanguard had taken 130 days, over 4 months, to cross some 265 miles of southern Iowa, averaging only about 2 miles per day. Here on both sides of the Missouri River, especially in present Nebraska at Winter Quarters, the Mormons spent the winter of 1846-47.

ACROSS NEBRASKA, WYOMING, AND UTAH IN 1847

In early January, 1847, the Pioneer Company began in earnest to get ready to start for the Rocky Mountains that spring. The traditional time, the "window," to head west from the Missouri River was sometime between April 15 and May 30.

Contrary to myth and popular belief, this 1847 trek of approximately 1,032 miles and 111 days—made by 143 men, 3 women, and 2 children—was not one long and unending "trail of tears" or a trial by fire. It was actually a great adventure.

The 1847 pioneer trek from "civilization to sundown" took a few days to get properly under way, as in 1846 when the Camp of Israel left Nauvoo. Heber C. Kimball moved three wagons out 4 miles on April 5. Subsequently other Pioneers followed. After they crossed the Elkhorn River, they converged several days later at their staging ground on the north bank of the Platte River near present Fremont, Nebraska. From there the Mormon Pioneers followed the Platte to near present Columbus, where they traveled westward along the Loup Fork of the Platte.

On April 24 they crossed the Loup near present Fullerton and went due south about 16 miles to again pick up the Platte. On May 1, just west of what is today Kearney, Nebraska, the Pioneers first sighted a herd of bison, a fact recorded in many journals.

On May 10, west of the confluence of the North and South Platte Rivers, several Pioneers made an instrument and attached it to a wagon wheel to measure miles traveled—the famous odometer.

West of Ash Hollow, a famous camping site on the Oregon Trail, the Mormons entered the broken lands of the lower North Platte River, and the terrain became increasingly more interesting and varied. In mid-May they crossed a short section of Nebraska's Sand Hills, where ruts may still be found.

On May 22 the Pioneers made camp near the most impressive topographic site along the Mormon Trail so far, a place the Mormons called Ancient Bluff Ruins, which consists of three separate and magnificently eroded formations. The place name remains to this day.

On May 26 they passed Chimney Rock—a principal milestone which, though only 452 miles from Winter Quarters, came to be considered sort of a halfway mark.

On Friday, May 28, they passed the future site of the famous Rebecca Winters grave and soon were opposite the massive formations of clay and sandstone called Scotts Bluff. The following day was Saturday, and Young convened a special meeting just east of today's Wyoming state line near present Henry, Nebraska. They went out on the bluffs and prayed for guidance.

That same day they spotted the pyramidal bulk of Laramie Peak looming regally above the "Black Hills," today's Laramie Mountains, the first western mountains seen by Platte Valley travelers. A day later they passed out of present Nebraska and came upon a wagon track which led them to Fort Laramie, 30 miles farther west.

While at Fort Laramie they rested their animals and themselves and prepared to pick up the Oregon Trail, the longest wagon road in history, the Main Street of the Old West, stretching over 2,000 miles from Independence, Missouri, to the Columbia River.

On Saturday, June 5, the Pioneers left Fort Laramie for the continental divide at South Pass and for Fort Bridger, which was 397 miles west. The Pioneers would be on the Oregon Trail for a little over a month.

On their first day out from Fort Laramie, they came to what is now called Mexican Hill, so steep, a story went, that if a tin cup fell out of a wagon it would land in front of the oxen. Two miles west of Mexican Hill is Register Cliff, and beyond that are probably the most dramatic trail ruts in the world–4 to 5 feet deep in solid rock–near present Guernsey, Wyoming.

On Sunday, June 13, while at their fording site on the North Platte River, frequently referred to as "Last Crossing," they established a ferry, both for the Saints who would follow and as a money-making venture.

When the Pioneers left Last Crossing on June 19, they quit the North Platte for good. From the Elkhorn River to Last Crossing they had followed its generally gentle valley for more than 600 miles. The easy part of the trek was over, as the next 50 miles would prove. The stretch from Last Crossing through Emigrant Gap, by Avenue of Rocks, Willow Springs, up Prospect Hill, and to the Sweetwater River near Independence Rock was especially difficult. It was a "Hell's Reach" of few and bad campsites, bad water, little grass, one steep hill, swamps, and stretches of alkali flats. But the Pioneers endured and lived to enjoy refreshing drafts of the Sweetwater River, which all Oregonians and Mormons followed for 93 miles to South Pass.

Like most travelers before and after them, the Pioneers stopped to climb the huge turtle-shaped Independence Rock,

and some carved or painted their initials or names into and on it. Four and a half miles west was the equally famous Devil's Gate, another popular resting place on the trail. It is a 1,500-foot-long, 370-foot-deep gap in a rocky spur through which flows the Sweetwater River.

West of Devil's Gate came Martin's Cove, the Split Rock Ruts, Three Crossings, the Ice Springs, the future site of the Willie Handcart Party grave, and South Pass.

On June 27 they crossed the flat, almost imperceptible, 7,750-foot-high continental divide at South Pass, the "Cumberland Gap" of the far west. At Pacific Springs, immediately west of South Pass, the Pioneers refreshed themselves and their animals. These famous springs, so named because their waters flowed to the Pacific Ocean, were the recognized beginning of the sprawling and ill-defined Oregon Territory.

By July 3 they were at the Green River, where they established another ferry. From there they passed Church Butte and, on the afternoon of July 7, finally arrived at Fort Bridger. This poorly built, ramshackle, log establishment on the Black's Fork of the Green River was put up in 1842 to service emigrants on the Oregon Trail.

The Pioneers tarried at this rather shabby fort just long enough to do some trading and repair their wagons. At 8 a.m. on Friday, July 9, the Pioneers quit the Oregon Trail, which there turned northwest, and began the last leg of their journey. The Mormons followed the Hastings Cutoff, a barely visible track through the Wasatch Range of the Rocky Mountains made by the Donner-Reed party of 1846. Even with the trailblazing done by that group, it took the Pioneers 14 days to traverse the 116 miles between Fort Bridger and the Salt Lake Valley.

Beyond Fort Bridger they entered a 90-mile-long natural highway, a chain of defiles which meandered through the forbidding Wasatch Range, before arriving in the Valley of the Great Salt Lake.

By noon on July 12, they reached the Needles, about a half mile east of the present Wyoming-Utah border. Here Young was suddenly stricken with tick or mountain fever. He remained ill for nearly 2 weeks, but finally, via the Hog's

Back, Little Emigration Canyon, Big Mountain, Little Mountain, and Emigration Canyon, entered the valley on July 24, the traditional pivot in Mormon history—everything is related to and from this date.

The event is commemorated today by the large granite "This Is the Place" monument at the mouth of Emigration Canyon, which honors the Pioneers and pre-Mormon explorers and trappers. Atop a huge shaft, thrusting up from the center of the base, stand larger-than-life-sized figures of Brigham Young, Heber C. Kimball, and Wilford Woodruff, serenely and eternally contemplating their work.

As the Pioneers crossed the 7,400-foot-high Big Mountain pass they entered the Salt Lake Valley of the Great Basin, their new homeland. The Great Basin is a vast and forbidding area of over 200,000 square miles, lying generally between the crests of the Sierra Nevada and the Wasatch Mountains.

The traveler may now go beyond this brief introduction and enjoy the power of place and spirit of locale by visiting the following 76 historic sites along the Mormon Pioneer National Historic Trail in Illinois, Iowa, Nebraska, Wyoming, and Utah.

Frederick Piercy – *Chimney Rock*

Part Three
Historic Sites and Markers Along the Mormon Trail

Note: Maps are not drawn to scale.

ILLINOIS

1. The Exodus to Greatness Historic Site/Marker:
This is the only historic trail site in Illinois. Travelers, however, should first visit the Nauvoo Restoration Inc. Visitors Center on Main Street.

Travelers should then drive to the foot of Parley Street, which is the approximate site where the Mormons crossed the Mississippi River into Iowa.

IOWA

2. Old Fort Des Moines Historic Site/Markers: From Nauvoo, travelers must cross the Mississippi River into Iowa via either Fort Madison or Keokuk, Iowa, and proceed to Montrose, directly opposite Nauvoo. Here on the banks of the Mississippi River, in present River Front Park, at the eastern end of Main Street, is where the Mormon Trail of 1846 properly begins. This small park is the site of the first Fort Des Moines (1834-37) and is marked by a bronze plaque set into a boulder at the south end of the park. After the 1838-39 expulsion from Missouri, some Mormons, including Brigham Young, temporarily lived in this abandoned old fort. The Iowa Mormon Trails Association has placed a wayside exhibit panel in this park.

A second panel, commemorating the miracle of the quails, is located north of Montrose in Linger Longer Park, off US 61 on the Mississippi River Road.

3. Sugar Creek Historic Site: Six miles west of Montrose, along Sugar Creek, on County Road J72 (watch for a bridge over this otherwise unmarked creek) is the site of the staging ground where in February 1846 the Mormons organized themselves for their trek across Iowa. There is no marker here.

4. Des Moines River Ford Historic Site/Markers: From Sugar Creek, proceed via Argyle, Donnellson, and Farmington to Bonaparte. (You may have to ask directions locally.) On March 5, 1846, the Pioneers forded the Des Moines River at Bonaparte, Iowa. This crossing is commemorated by a sign and an Iowa Mormon Trails Association wayside exhibit in the city park on the Bonaparte side of the bridge, over the river on County Road J40.

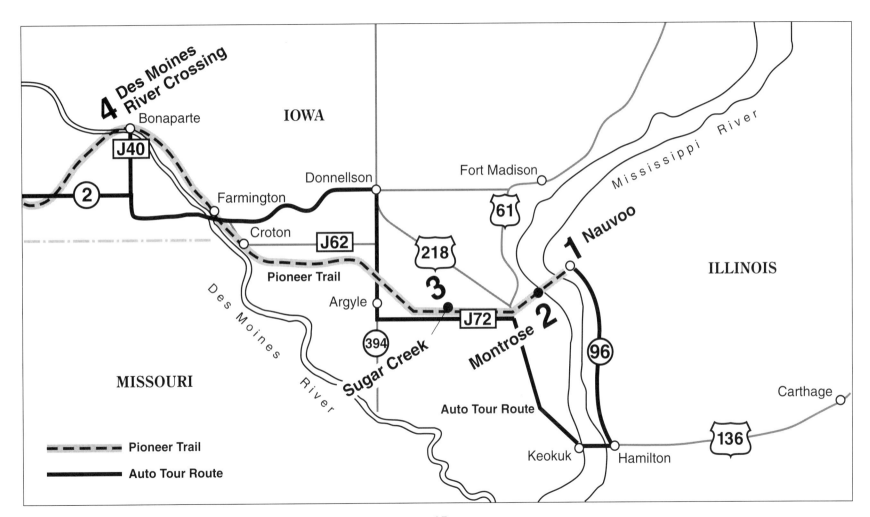

There is another wayside exhibit at the courthouse in nearby Keosauqua commemorating concerts that Pitt's Brass Band played there in 1846.

5. Davis County Wayside Exhibits: Two new wayside exhibits have been developed along the Mormon Trail in Davis County. The first panel is located on the grounds of the Davis County Historical Complex in Bloomfield. A fully restored log cabin, which was built by the Mormon Pioneers as they made their way west, has been moved to this complex.

The second panel marks the division of the northern and southern routes of the Mormon Trail and is located in a small park in downtown Drakesville on IA 273.

6. Chariton River Crossing/Marker: A wayside exhibit has been erected overlooking the Chariton River Crossing. However, the site is remote and difficult to find. Ask locally for directions or try the following: From Drakesville go south to IA 2, proceed west to IA 202, and turn south 3 miles to Moulton. Turn right on County Road J51. Go 4 miles to the Sedan Bottoms. Go 1 more mile and turn left at the first T-junction. Then take another left.

7. Locust Creek Historic Campsite/Markers: Here, on April 15, 1846, William Clayton wrote the words to the most famous of all Mormon hymns, "Come, Come, Ye Saints." A marker commemorating this event was erected here in July 1990 and is located at the entrance to the Tharp Cemetery. At the time the hymn was written, the Pioneer camp was located along the ridge immediately west of the Tharp Cemetery. This ridge divides two branches of Locust Creek. A wayside exhibit was recently erected at this location.

This site, one of the most important in Iowa, is not easy to find. Proceed west via IA 2 to Corydon, Wayne County. Here travelers should first visit the exhibit dedicated to this event in the Wayne County Pioneer Trails Museum on IA 2 (See site 8). Then ask locally for directions some 15 miles to the Tharp Cemetery.

8. Wayne County Pioneer Trails Museum: A wayside exhibit discussing women's roles in the Mormon migration is located at the Wayne County Pioneer Trails Museum in Corydon. This fine museum also contains the impressive "Come, Come Ye Saints" exhibit, including maps, photos,

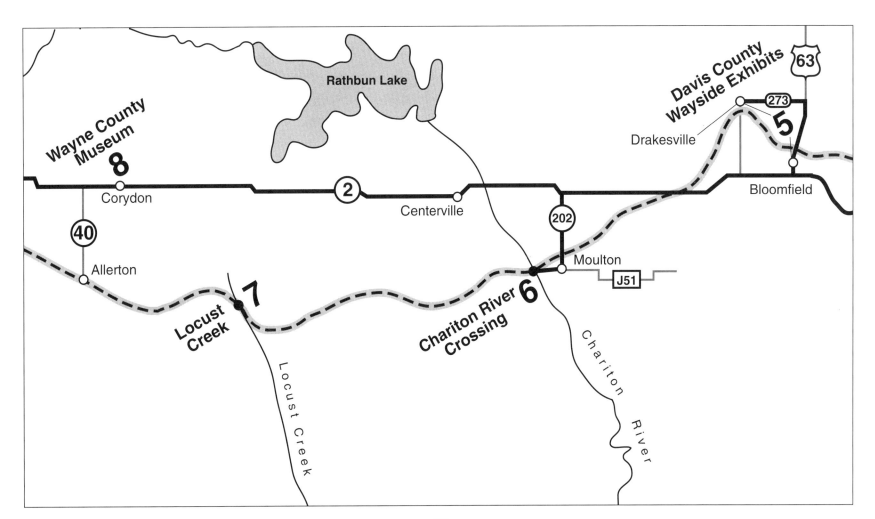

Rathbun Lake

Wayne County Museum **8**

Corydon

40

Allerton

2

Centerville

202

Moulton

J51

Davis County Wayside Exhibits

63

273

Drakesville

5

Bloomfield

Locust Creek **7**

Chariton River Crossing **6**

Locust Creek

Chariton River

illustrations, and a full size replica of a family with covered wagon and oxen.

9. Garden Grove Historic Site/Markers: From Corydon, proceed west to IA 204, turn north to County Road J20, and turn left to Garden Grove. In the town park is a small marker commemorating the founding of this community by the Pioneers during April 1846. Here the Mormons built a semipermanent camp for the benefit of those who would follow.

One mile straight west of this marker, on a county road, is small, 3-acre Trailside Historic Park. Just to the north of an A-frame picnic shelter is a fenced plot enclosing a metal marker on a sandstone slab. This marker commemorates "The Latter-day Saints at Garden Grove" and those who are buried in that park. Two wayside exhibits describe the founding and development of the camp. In recent times members of the Iowa Mormon Trails Association have studied the old camp site and have marked where Mormon cabins and a graveyard appear to have been located.

10. Clarke County Sites: From 1994-1996 local students mapped 4 1/2 miles of Mormon Trail ruts in Clarke County. The Seven Mile Campsite is located west of Murray, off US 34, on private land, but the owner welcomes visitors. Ask locally for directions to these sites

A wayside exhibit, discussing the development of the Mormon Trail as a transportation corridor, is located in Murray on 5th Street, between Grant and Maple. A one-room school and Mormon Trail exhibits can also be seen at this location.

11. Mount Pisgah Historic Site/Markers: From Murray return south to US 34, turn west about 6 miles, go north 2 miles on US 169 and follow signs to Mount Pisgah. The road twists a bit, and you will have to pass through a farmer's yard to reach the cemetery—*drive slowly.*

The original community was located on the slope and flatlands east of this spot. The cemetery extended down the hill to the west, north, and south beyond the railroad tracks. Like Garden Grove, Mount Pisgah was a semipermanent camp on the trail, for the benefit of the Mormons who

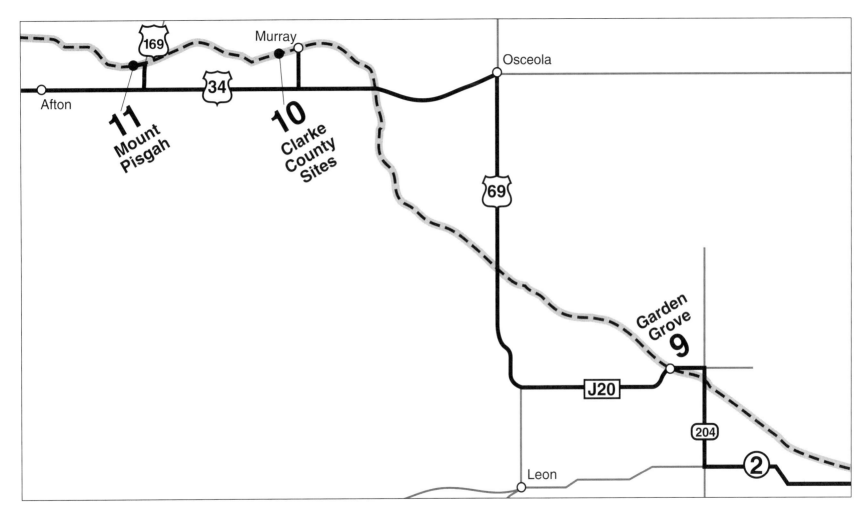

followed the Pioneers west. Mount Pisgah was a stopping place for westward-bound Mormons until 1852, when the last of the Latter-day Saints left that camp and moved west to the Missouri River.

There is little left of the old campsite, which today is a small, 9-acre park with informative signs and historical markers. In 1888 the Mormons erected a monument honoring their dead who rest in the adjacent cemetery. This monument may have been the first marker to a historic site erected in Iowa. A reproduction log cabin and a wayside exhibit have recently been erected on the site.

12. Three Mile Lake Park Wayside Exhibit: Another wayside exhibit, which discusses the naming of creeks in the area, has been placed in Three Mile Lake Park west of Mount Pisgah. Go 3 miles north of Afton on County Road P53 (Creamery Road) and 1/2 mile west on Three Mile Campground Road.

13. Orient/Marker: A wayside exhibit "Growing Up on the Trail" has been placed at the corner of First and Broad streets in the Town of Orient on IA 25. Across the street from the panel, an 1894 bank building is being restored as a historical museum, which will contain Mormon Trail exhibits.

14. Mormon Trail Park: Two miles east of Bridgewater, Adair County, on a county road, is the 160-acre Mormon Trail Park and Morman [sic] Lake. (Follow signs.) This pleasant little park commemorates the old Mormon Trail, which ran about 1 mile to the south.

To reach Bridgewater from Orient take County Road G61 west to County Road N51 and turn north. Ask locally for directions.

A short walk through a section of restored prairie in this park allows the visitor to experience the Iowa prairies as the Mormon Pioneers saw them. A wayside exhibit sits at the start of the trail.

15. Mormon Trail Ruts Historic Site: Some of the very few extant Mormon Trail ruts in Iowa are found near this Mormon Trail Park. They are located north of County Road G61, on the property of Mr. Jacob Pote. The deeply eroded ruts, on his private pasture ground, run east and west for about 0.25 miles. *Permission to visit the ruts must be obtained.*

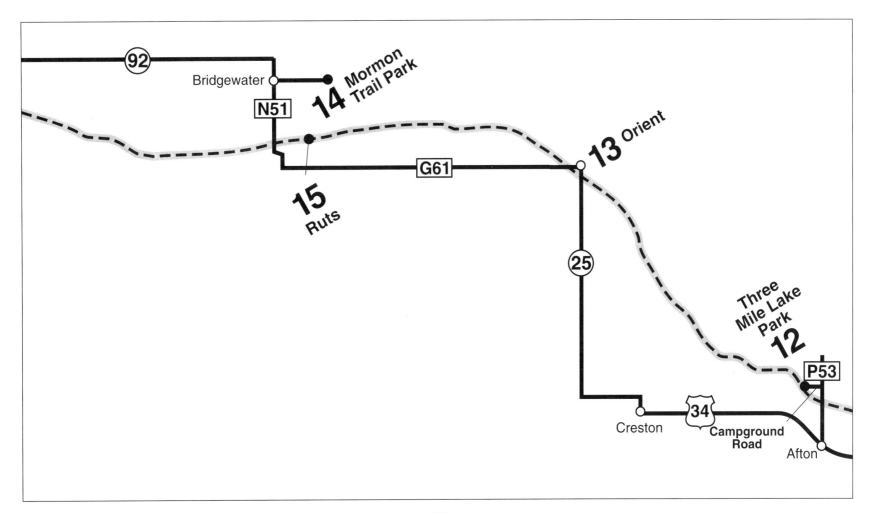

92

Bridgewater

N51

14 Mormon Trail Park

15 Ruts

G61

13 Orient

25

Three Mile Lake Park

12

P53

Creston

34

Campground Road

Afton

16. Junction of Pioneer Trail and Handcart Trail/ Markers: This historic junction took place near present Lewis, Cass County. It was here that the handcart companies from Iowa City, Iowa, picked up the Pioneer route of 1846.

To reach Lewis from Bridgewater, return to IA 92, turn west to US 71, turn north to County Road G43, and turn west to Lewis. There is a marker in the town park.

The actual site of the junction is about 1 mile west on Minnesota Avenue, at the site of an old Indian Town—a Pottawattamie settlement on the east bank of the Nishnabotna River.

Two new wayside exhibits have been installed in the area by the Iowa Mormon Trails Association. The first is located at the Ferry House, just west of Lewis at 701 West Minnesota Avenue. The second is at the Hitchcock House. Continue west on Minnesota Avenue for about 1 mile and south 1/2 mile. Watch for signs.

17. Macedonia Historic Site/Markers: From Lewis, take US 6 and US 59 south to Macedonia. This small town, just west off US 59 in southern Pottawattamie County, was an early Mormon settlement. A 10,000 pound red granite boulder, commemorating Old Macedonia, is located just west of town on the north side of County Road G66. A wayside exhibit on the founding of Macedonia is nearby.

18. West Nishnabotna River Crossing: One mile west of Macedonia, on County Road G66, is Old Towne Park, an undeveloped eight acre park near a temporary 1850 Mormon settlement. The site became known as the Mormon Trail Crossing.

19. Mosquito Creek Campsite/Markers: From Macedonia, take US 59 south to County Road H12, and turn west to US 275. Then go north to the Iowa School for the Deaf, near the junction of US 275 and IA 92. This is the general area of the first Mormon camp in the Council Bluffs area. On the campus are several markers. One commemorates the Mormon Battalion, which served in the war with Mexico, 1846-48. A second discusses the Grand Encampment.

20. Council Bluffs Historic Marker: From the School for the Deaf, proceed to Bayliss Park on South Main Street (IA 192) in downtown Council Bluffs. At the north end of this park is a

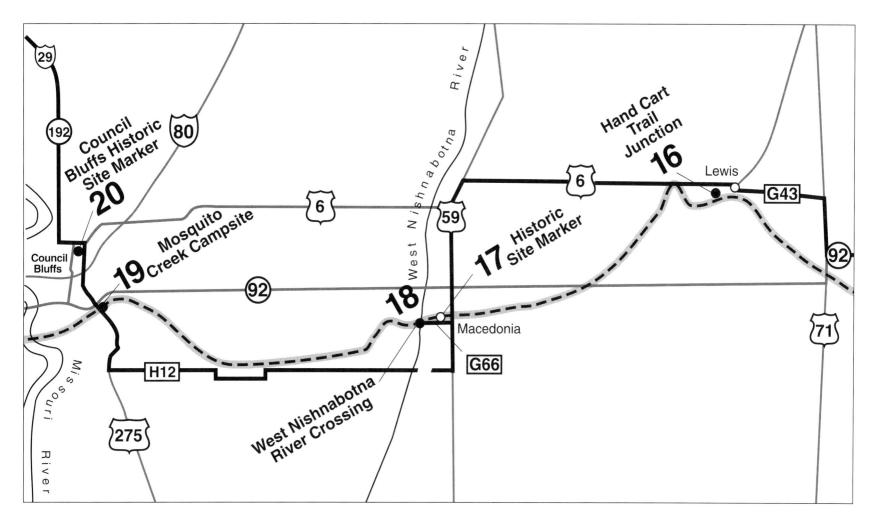

Council Bluffs Historic Site Marker **20**

Council Bluffs

19 Mosquito Creek Campsite

Hand Cart Trail Junction **16**

Lewis

17 Historic Site Marker

18

Macedonia

West Nishnabotna River Crossing

West Nishnabotna River

Missouri River

29

192

80

6

59

6

G43

92

92

71

92

H12

275

G66

bronze marker commemorating the Mormon Trail's passage through Council Bluffs.

21. The Kanesville Tabernacle Historic Site/Visitor Center: This recently reconstructed building is where Brigham Young was sustained as the second president of the Mormon Church in 1847. It is located on Broadway in Council Bluffs. There is a small visitor center nearby.

22. The Mormon Pioneer Memorial Bridge Historic Site: To reach this bridge, take I-29 about 10 miles north from Bayliss Park, and turn west on I-680. This bridge, dedicated in 1953, commemorates an important Mormon ferry site, which was used for travel between the Council Bluffs area and Winter Quarters, present-day north Omaha. (There is a historical marker to this bridge and ferry site, but it is on the Nebraska side. See Historic Site 23.)

NEBRASKA

23. Mormon Pioneer Memorial Bridge Historic Site/Marker: (For the location and significance of this site, see Historic Site 22.) The historic marker is on the grounds

of the old Florence Bank at 8502 North 30th Street, in north Omaha near the Nebraska end of the bridge.

24. Winter Quarters Area Historic Sites: Today in the area of old Winter Quarters are several historic sites and markers that commemorate Cutler's Park, Winter Quarters, the Mormon Cemetery, the 1846 Mormon Council House, and the old Mormon Mill. There are also streets named Young Street, Mormon Street, and Mormon Bridge Road, and a Mormon Trail Center, all located in the general area of 30th and State Streets. (This part of present Omaha has been known variously as Winter Quarters, Florence, and North Omaha.)

25. Winter Quarters Historic Site/Marker: In the southern end of Florence Park, at 30th and State Streets, is a Nebraska Historical Marker telling the story of Winter Quarters. This area sheltered more than 3,000 people during the winter of 1846-47 and was used by emigrating Mormons until 1852, when it was abandoned.

26. Winter Quarters Cemetery Historic Site/ Markers: This site is in old Florence, now north Omaha, at

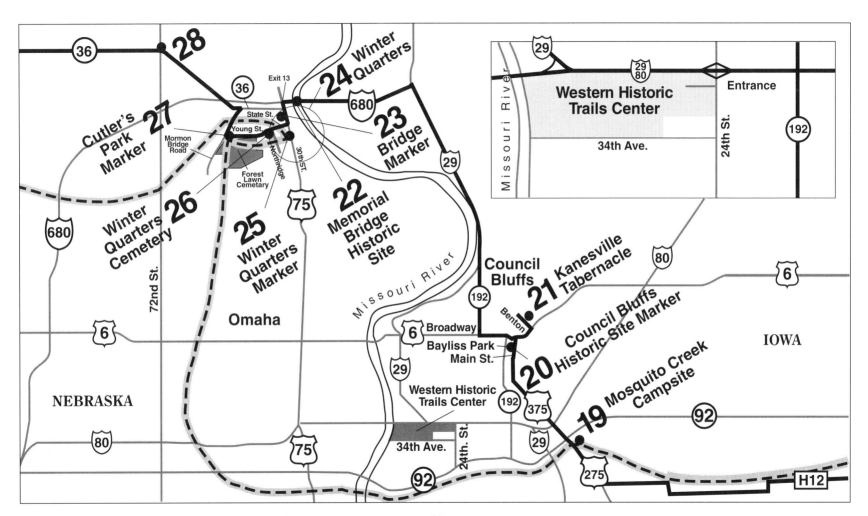

36 28

36 Exit 13

24 Winter Quarters

680

27 Cutler's Park Marker

State St.

Young St.

Mormon Bridge Road

Northridge

30th ST.

23 Bridge Marker

29

Forest Lawn Cemetary

680

26 Winter Quarters Cemetery

75

22 Memorial Bridge Historic Site

72nd St.

25 Winter Quarters Marker

Missouri River

Council Bluffs

21 Kanesville Tabernacle

80

Omaha

Benton

6

192

6 Broadway

6

20 Council Bluffs Historic Site Marker

IOWA

NEBRASKA

29

Bayliss Park Main St.

Western Historic Trails Center

192

375

19 Mosquito Creek Campsite

92

80

75

34th. Ave.

24th. St.

29

275

92

92

H12

Missouri River

29

29 80

Western Historic Trails Center

Entrance

24th St.

192

34th Ave.

the intersection of State and Northridge. Many who died at Winter Quarters were buried here during 1846-52. There are seven markers in and near the cemetery, including some of the finest works of sculpture produced by the Mormon church. Across the street from the cemetery is a new Mormon Trail Center with interpretive exhibits on the history of the entire trail.

27. Cutler's Park Historic Site/Marker: This site and marker are located on Mormon Bridge Road, just north of the entrance to the Forest Lawn Cemetery. Before the establishment of Winter Quarters in September 1846, this short-lived community was selected by Alpheus Cutler as the Mormon headquarters in present Nebraska. It is known today as "Nebraska's First City." Mormon Bridge Road can be intersected by driving west from Winter Quarters (Site 26) on Young Street. (Turn right to see the marker.)

28. Mormon Pioneer Camp Historic Site/Marker: About 4 miles west of the Mormon Pioneer Memorial Bridge is the first monument to the exodus across Nebraska. It is located on Old NE 36, near the intersection of NE 36 and Seventy-second Street, at the southern boundary of the North Omaha Airport. (Turn north on Seventy-second Street and take the first turn to the right.) The marker commemorates the first Pioneer camp west of Winter Quarters on April 15, 1847.

29. Elkhorn River Crossing: The exact site of this crossing, the first natural obstacle in Nebraska, is not certain. Some claim it was approximately where US 6 crosses this river near Waterloo, Douglas County. The most recent research, however, suggests it was to the north, where NE 36 crosses this river. A wayside exhibit is to be placed in a park west of the river and south of the highway. A small, one foot high and hard to find, marker is located just south of the "T" intersection of 240th street and NE 36.

30. Liberty Pole Camp and Staging Ground Historic Site/Markers: Once across the Elkhorn, the Pioneers headed for the broad and gentle valley, or flood plain, of the Platte River. (From the Elkhorn River go west to US 275 and turn north towards Fremont.) This staging ground is located on a former bend in the river near State Lakes Avenue, just west of Fremont, on the road to Fremont Lakes State

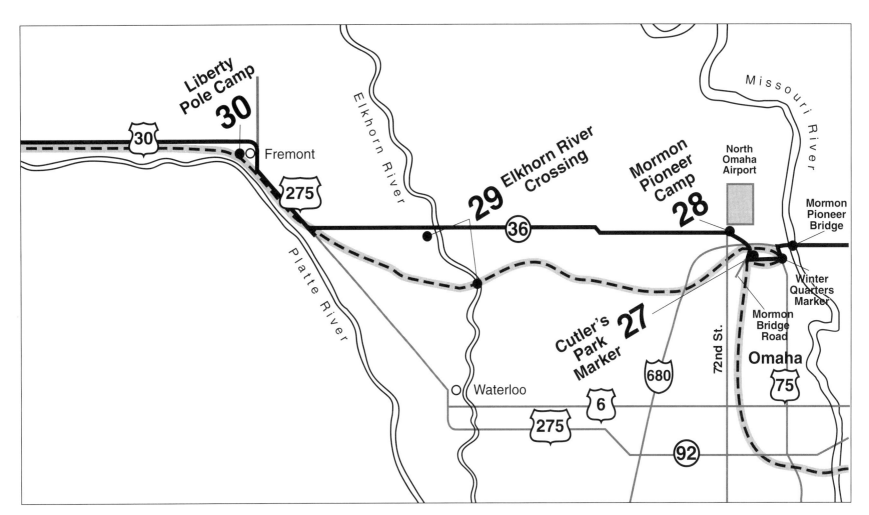

Liberty
Pole Camp
30

Elkhorn River

Missouri River

North
Omaha
Airport

29 Elkhorn River
Crossing

Mormon
Pioneer
Camp
28

Mormon
Pioneer
Bridge

Fremont

Platte River

Cutler's
Park
Marker **27**

Winter
Quarters
Marker

Mormon
Bridge
Road

72nd St.

Omaha

Waterloo

27

Recreation Area. A reconstructed Liberty Pole, made from a trimmed cottonwood tree, has been erected here. A new marker will also be placed at this site.

There are three others in the vicinity. The first is 100 yards east of the intersection of US 275 and NE 36; the second is in Barnard Park in Fremont, between Irving and Clarkson Streets on Military Avenue; and the third is 4 miles west of Barnard Park, on the south side of US 30, at the entrance to the Fremont Lakes State Recreation Area.

31. Genoa Historic Site/Marker: The Mormons founded this community in Nance County in 1857, as a temporary way station on their trail west. It was used until 1859. The community is on NE 22, about 20 miles west of Columbus. The marker is in the Genoa City Park, at the west end of the community.

32. Loup Ford of 1847 Historic Site: This pioneer ford is south of NE 22, about 4 miles east of Fullerton. The ford is on private ground and is not marked. However, a wayside exhibit will be placed at the Pawnee village site, approximately 7 miles west of Genoa on NE 22.

En route the traveler might wish to stop at the Mormon Island State Wayside Area located at the Grand Island exit off the west bound lane of I-80.

33. Murdock Site/Ruts: The Hall County Historical Society owns this small 2 acre piece of land with pristine wagon ruts and plans to erect a wayside exhibit here. The site is west of Grand Island and is not easy to locate. I recommend driving west on US 30 to Alda and taking a section line (county) road exactly 2 miles south to another section line road. The site is on the north-west corner of that intersection.

34. Sand Hills Historic Trail Ruts: These ruts are located west of North Platte and 3 1/2 miles north of US 30 at Sutherland, Lincoln County, immediately to the northeast of the Sutherland Bridge over the North Platte River. They are among the few, as well as some of the best, Mormon Trail ruts in Nebraska. *The ruts are on private land and one must secure permission to visit them.* Current research suggests that it was just west of here that the famous "odometer" was developed and tested, while others claim it was on land now occupied by the North Platte Airport.

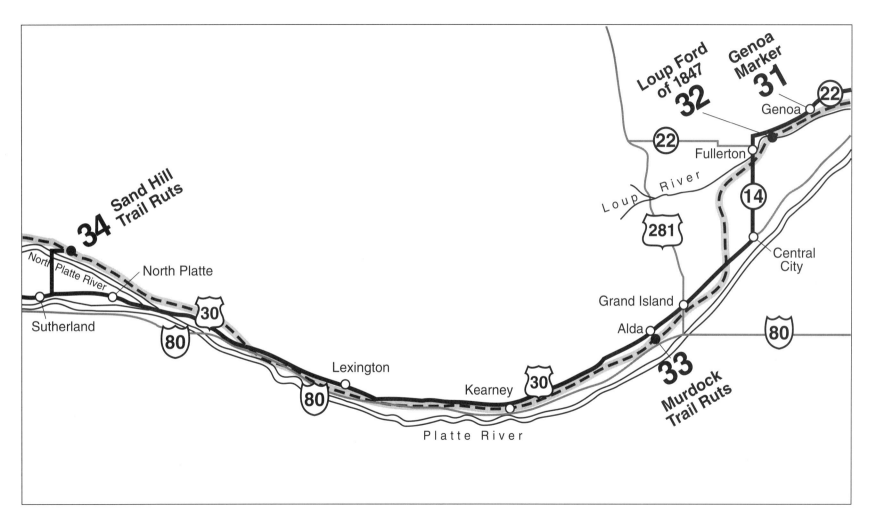

34 Sand Hill Trail Ruts

North Platte River

North Platte

Sutherland

Lexington

Kearney

Platte River

Loup Ford of 1847 **32**

Genoa Marker **31**

Genoa

Fullerton

Loup River

Central City

Grand Island

Alda

33 Murdock Trail Ruts

35. Indian Lookout Point Historic Landmark: This landmark is located 2 miles west of Lisco, Garden County, to the north of US 26. The Pioneers called it Frog's Head Bluff. Many Mormons climbed this promontory to take their bearings and to try to spot Chimney Rock to the west.

36. Ancient Bluff Ruins: This formation is located 8 miles west of Lisco, north of US 26. These three erosional remnant buttes were named by English Mormon immigrants who thought they resembled castles in their homeland. On Sunday, May 23, 1847, Mormon leaders climbed the highest bluff, wrote their names on a buffalo skull, and placed it at the southwest corner. *This landmark is on private land and one must secure permission to visit the site.*

37. Ancient Bluff Ruins Historic Ruts/Marker: In connection with, but separate from, the bluffs is a very short, less than 100 feet long, set of well defined trail ruts. They can be found three-tenths of a mile east of the ranch road that leads into the bluff area, just to the north of US 26. *The ruts are on private land; please secure permission from the owner before visiting the ruts.* The marker is about 1 1/2 miles east of the site.

38. Rebecca Winters Grave/Marker: Three miles east of Scottsbluff, Scotts Bluff County, along US 26, is a pullout with a Nebraska historical marker where the Belt Line Road crosses the Burlington Northern Santa Fe Railroad.

This famous grave is one of the few known graves of the approximately 6,000 Mormons who died crossing the plains. The grave has been moved from its original location, about one-quarter of a mile west of here, to the area of the pullout.

39. Prayer Circle Bluffs Historic Site: Near Henry, Scotts Bluff County, on US 26. These low, sandy bluffs are about one mile east of Henry. They can be reached by a service road, but the visit is not worth the effort, for the bluffs are visible from US 26 to the south. It was here on May 30, 1847, that Brigham Young called a special prayer circle on behalf of the Pioneers traveling with him, those following behind, and others remaining in Winter Quarters. A wayside exhibit for this site is under consideration.

WYOMING

40. Fort Laramie/Marker/Ruts: Before visiting the fort, one should stop in the community of Fort Laramie on

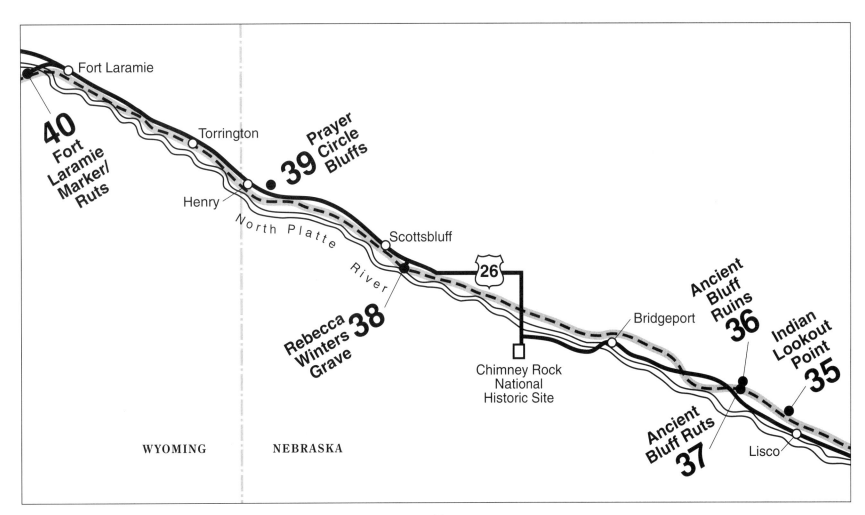

40
Fort Laramie Marker/ Ruts

Fort Laramie

Torrington

39 Prayer Circle Bluffs

Henry

North Platte River

Scottsbluff

Rebecca Winters Grave **38**

🛡26

Chimney Rock National Historic Site

Bridgeport

Ancient Bluff Ruins **36**

Indian Lookout Point **35**

Ancient Bluff Ruts **37**

Lisco

WYOMING

NEBRASKA

31

US 26. There is a visitor center and marker there. The historic fort is easily reached from the west end of town by turning south on WY 160 and following it 3 miles to the fort. The buildings that remain at Fort Laramie today date largely from the 1870s and 80s.

Here the Mormons crossed the North Platte River and picked up the Oregon Trail, which they followed 396 miles west to Fort Bridger. Some excellent and recently discovered trail ruts may be visited by driving west for about 1 mile (towards Guernsey) on a gravel road which starts across from the cemetery near the fort. Watch for a sign or ask at the visitor center for a map and informational handout on these ruts.

41. Register Cliff/Marker: This famous site, covered with names from trail days, is located 2 miles southeast, across the North Platte River, from the center of the community of Guernsey. Guernsey may be reached by continuing west on the same gravel road used to visit the ruts near Fort Laramie. *In bad weather travelers are advised to go via US 26.*

42. Guernsey Oregon-California-Mormon Trail Ruts/ Marker: One and one-half miles beyond Register Cliff are some of the most dramatic ruts of any trail in the world—cut four to five feet deep through solid rock. Follow road signs to these ruts.

43. Ayres Natural Bridge Park: This beautiful natural bridge, with water running under it, is not directly on the Mormon Trail, but many Mormons rode over to see it. Take US 26 west from Guernsey to I-25 and turn north. Watch for the Ayres Park sign about 10 miles west of Douglas.

44. Mormon Ferry Site: This historic site is located at rebuilt old Fort Caspar on Fort Caspar Road in Casper. This ferry, considered to have been the first commercial ferry on the North Platte River, was established by the Mormon Pioneers in June 1847. Built in 1858, the reconstructed old fort is also worth visiting. There is an excellent Mormon exhibit in the fort museum and a full sized replica of the original Mormon ferry on the fort grounds.

45. Emigrant Gap Historic Landmark/Marker: This gap is along Poison Spider Road, 10 miles west of Casper. Poison Spider Road turns west off US 26 in the small town of Mills, just west of Casper. Most travelers on the Oregon-California-Mormon Trail passed through this shallow gap in

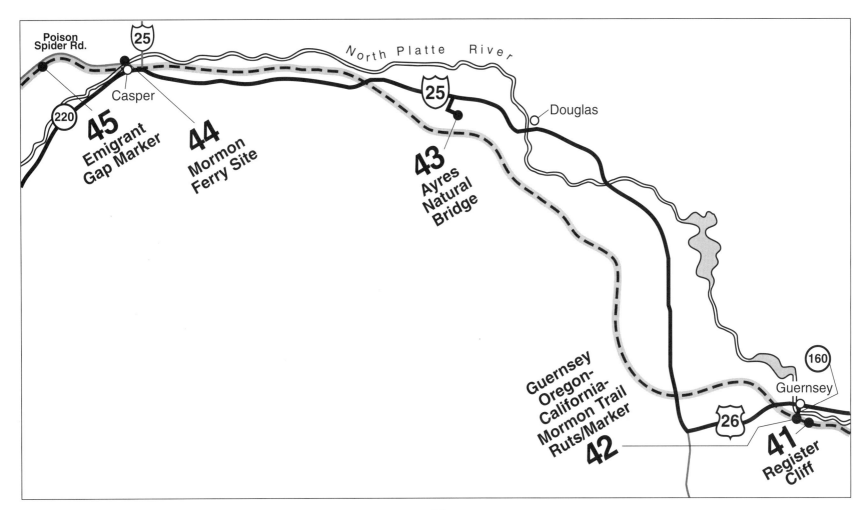

Poison
Spider Rd.

25

Casper

45
Emigrant
Gap Marker

220

44
Mormon
Ferry Site

North Platte River

25

Douglas

43
Ayres
Natural
Bridge

Guernsey
Oregon-
California-
Mormon Trail
Ruts/Marker

42

160

Guernsey

26

41
Register
Cliff

the Emigrant Gap Ridge. There is a Bureau of Land Management (BLM) informational pullout here.

Some trail students believe that the original Pioneers of 1847 went to the south of Emigrant Gap, generally following the river to present Bessemer Bend, also known as the Red Buttes crossing. This is located 6 miles west of Casper on WY 220. A BLM interpretive site is located near the river.

46. Avenue of Rocks Historic Landmark: *(Sites 46-48 are located on a desolate gravel road with no services of any kind for 35 miles. In bad weather travelers are advised to drive to site 49 via WY 220 out of Casper.)* What remains of the Avenue of Rocks historic site is 6 miles west of Emigrant Gap on County Road 319, off Poison Spider Road. Most of the avenue has been destroyed by road builders. Some emigrant signatures may still be found in the area.

47. Willow Springs Historic Site: These springs are 9 miles west of Avenue of Rocks *on private land; please ask permission to enter.* They provided the only good water and campground for Mormon emigrants between the Platte and Sweetwater Rivers. The springs can be seen north of the road near some abandoned ranch buildings. (It is not necessary to enter the property to see the springs.)

48. Prospect (Ryan) Hill Landmark/Marker: One mile beyond Willow Springs. This 400-foot-high hill was originally called Prospect Hill because from its summit emigrants could see the gentle valley of the Sweetwater River, giving them hope, or good prospects, for better water and an easier road. Excellent trail ruts may be seen about a quarter mile northwest of the present road. There is a BLM informational pullout here.

49. Independence Rock/Visitor Center: Twenty-two miles beyond Prospect Hill, on WY 220. Near this rock, one of the most famous landmarks on the Oregon-California-Mormon Trail, emigrants picked up the gentle, beneficent Sweetwater River, which they followed west for about 93 miles to the Continental Divide at South Pass. Here are informational signs, many names carved and painted on the rock, and several bronze plaques, one of which commemorates the Mormon passage.

50. Devil's Gate Historic Landmark/Markers: Six miles west of Independence Rock, on WY 220. This famous

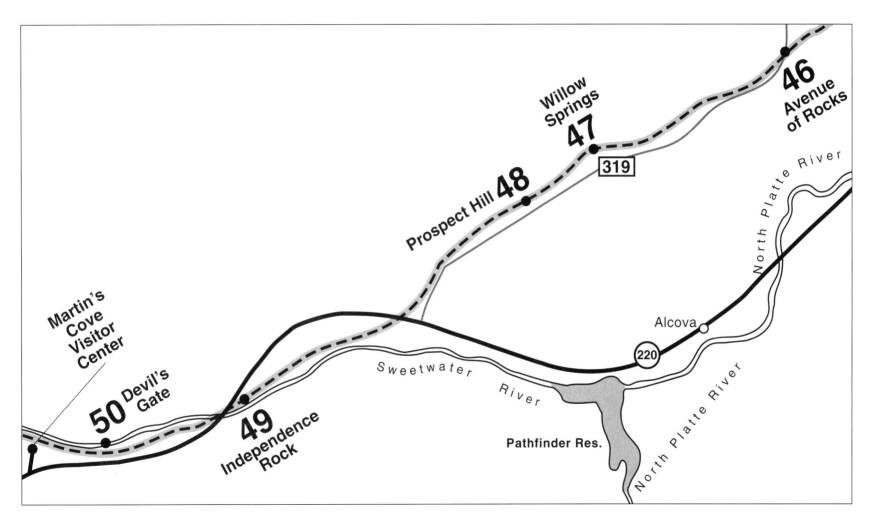

Willow Springs **47**

46 Avenue of Rocks

Prospect Hill **48**

319

North Platte River

Martin's Cove Visitor Center

Alcova

220

50 Devil's Gate

49 Independence Rock

Sweetwater River

Pathfinder Res.

North Platte River

North Platte River

landmark is a 370-foot-high and 1,500-foot-long cleft, or water gap, through the Sweetwater Rocks. There is a BLM interpretive site with 7 wayside exhibits just south of Devil's Gate on WY 220.

51. Martin's Cove/Marker: To reach this famous site continue west on WY 220 and watch for a "Mormon Handcart Visitor's Center" sign. In 1997 the Mormon Church opened a visitor's center in the renovated Sun Ranch house with interpretive exhibits explaining the story of the Willie and Martin handcart companies.

The cove is the place where the Martin Handcart Company was snowed in during a November 1856 blizzard and where help from Salt Lake City finally reached them. The cove can be reached by taking a hiking trail from the visitor's center. There is a marker there.

52. Split Rock Mountain/Markers: This famous "gun sight" trail landmark, some 15 miles west of the Martin's Cove area, in the Rattlesnake Range, can be seen to the north of US 287. Look for a large cleft in the mountains. There is a BLM interpretive site with 5 markers in the area.

53. Ice Springs Historic Area/Marker: Nine miles west of Jeffrey City, on US 287. Under these famous springs emigrants found ice in the summer.

54. Willie Handcart Company Grave Site/Marker: This site is located 7 miles south of Atlantic City, which is just off WY 28. Ask locally for the gravel road out of town to the south, and then follow signs to the gravesite, which has been interpreted by the Mormon Church. This handcart company, a companion of the Martin company, was caught in the same 1856 blizzard before they were rescued.

55. South Pass Historic Site: West of Atlantic City, on WY 28. This gentle pass through the Rocky Mountains is considered the "Cumberland Gap of the Far West," beyond which, in 1847, commenced the fabled land of Oregon. Just to the east of this pass there is a rest area near a bridge over the Sweetwater River. Four miles beyond the rest area, just south of WY 28, is a BLM Interpretive Site and Overlook concerning the South Pass area, which provides an excellent view of the pass and Pacific Springs.

56. Pacific Springs Historic Site: These springs are located *on private land* four miles west of South Pass, off

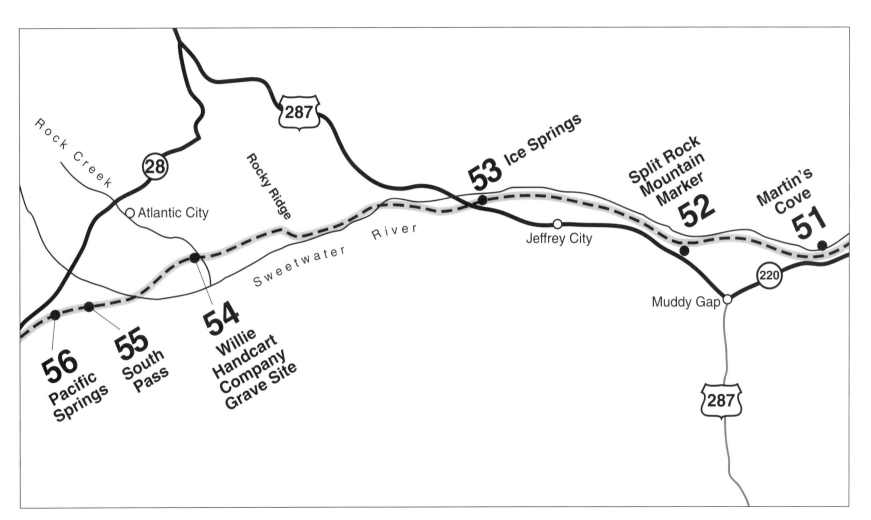

Rock Creek

287

28

Rocky Ridge

Atlantic City

Sweetwater River

53 Ice Springs

Split Rock
Mountain
Marker
52

Martin's
Cove
51

Jeffrey City

220

Muddy Gap

54
Willie
Handcart
Company
Grave Site

56
Pacific
Springs

55
South
Pass

287

WY 28. *Please secure permission before visiting the site.* This famous campsite was so named because this was the first water seen by westering Americans that flowed to the Pacific Ocean. The site is very difficult to reach by passenger cars. It can, however, be seen clearly from the South Pass Interpretive Site and Overlook mentioned above.

Six miles beyond the exhibit site, to the north of WY 28, is the so-called "False Parting of the Ways" BLM marker. The actual parting of the ways—where the Sublette Cutoff left the main Oregon Trail—is some 15 miles northeast of Farson on rough and unmarked ranch roads.

57. Simpson's Hollow Historic Site/Markers: This BLM site with two interpretive signs is located 10 miles southwest of Farson, to the north of WY 28. Here on October 6, 1857, Mormon guerrillas burned some U.S. Army supply wagons during the so-called "Utah War" of 1857-58.

58. Green River Mormon Ferry Site/Markers: This BLM interpretive site is located 28 miles southwest of Farson, where WY 28 crosses the Green River. The Mormons established this ferry in 1847 to help subsequent Mormons and also as a commercial venture. There are four historic markers here. The site is also known as the Lombard Ferry.

59. Church Butte Historic Landmark: This magnificently eroded butte, 10 miles southwest of Granger, Uinta County, acquired its name because some Mormons were supposed to have held church services here at one time.

It is on *private land* adjacent to the old Lincoln Highway, which is now kept up mainly by ranch and oil interests. *Be prepared to drive 27 utterly desolate miles between Granger and Lyman. Ask for directions locally.*

60. Fort Bridger/Markers: Six miles beyond Lyman (BUS I-80) is Fort Bridger, the second most important fort on the old Mormon Pioneer Trail, the first one being Fort Laramie (see Historic Site 40). Here the main Oregon Trail (which the Pioneers of 1847 picked up nearly 400 miles back at Fort Laramie) turns northwest, and the Mormons continued west about 100 miles on the year-old track of the Donner-Reed party into present Salt Lake City.

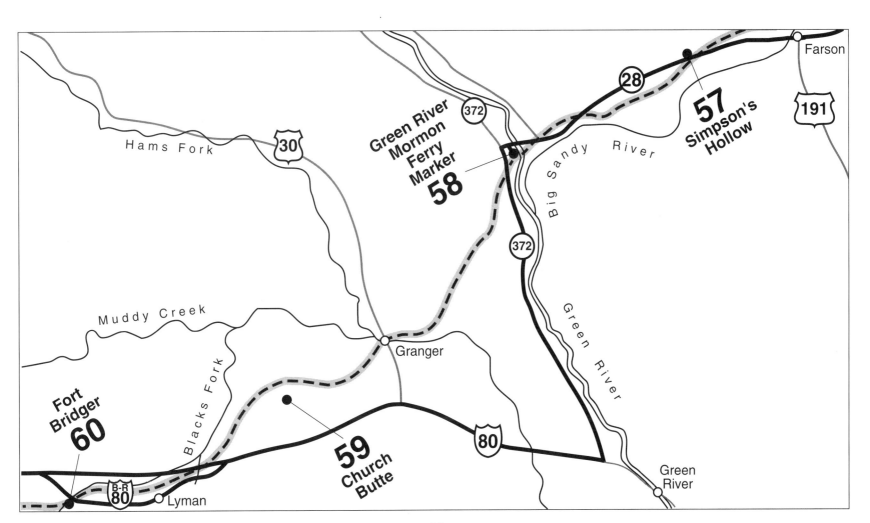

Hams Fork

US 30

372

Green River
Mormon
Ferry
Marker
58

28

57
Simpson's
Hollow

Farson

US 191

Big Sandy River

372

Muddy Creek

Granger

Green River

Fort
Bridger
60

Blacks Fork

59
Church
Butte

I 80

B-R 80

Lyman

Green River

A scaled down reconstruction of the original fort can be seen, and a visit to the fort's museum is recommended. A small section of a rebuilt cobblestone wall, erected by the Mormons, can also be seen.

61. The Needles Historic Landmark: This site is located near the Wyoming-Utah state line. The landmark is a 7,600-foot-high formation of conglomerate rock. It was just east of this formation, in July 1847, where Brigham Young was taken sick with tick or mountain fever and, therefore, entered the Valley of the Great Salt Lake 2 days after the vanguard.

In Evanston, exit south off I-80 on the Yellow Creek/ Overthrust Road, and drive some 8 miles. The formation is east of the road on *private land.*

UTAH

There are two ways to proceed west into Utah from the Needles. One is to return to Evanston and go west on I-80. The other is to take an old, unmarked ranch road, located immediately west of the Needles, and drive 4 miles to an intersect with I-80 at a railroad siding called Wahsatch.

62. Echo Canyon Historic Site/Marker: The 70-mile-long trail in Utah winds through a string of canyons in the Wasatch Range of the Rocky Mountains, the most important of which is 25-mile-long Echo Canyon.

There are some "Utah War" breastworks from 1857-58 high up on the north wall. They are positioned at the canyon's narrowest point, 20.4 miles down I-80 from Wahsatch.

Near here, on old US 30, is what is left of an old wooden marker, erected by the Utah State Road Commission. To reach old US 30, exit I-80 at Exit #180, signed Emory, 13 miles down the canyon from Wahsatch.

63. Echo Canyon Welcome Center/Marker: This center is near the mouth of Echo Canyon on westbound I-80 and interpretive panels are located at the center.

64. Witches Rocks Natural Formation: These strangely eroded formations, geologically known as "hoodoos," were often commented on by emigrants. They can be seen to the east of I-84, between Echo and Henefer. *Important: Leave I-84 at Exit 115!*

65. Henefer Park/Markers: A kiosk containing three interpretive panels, which commemorate the California,

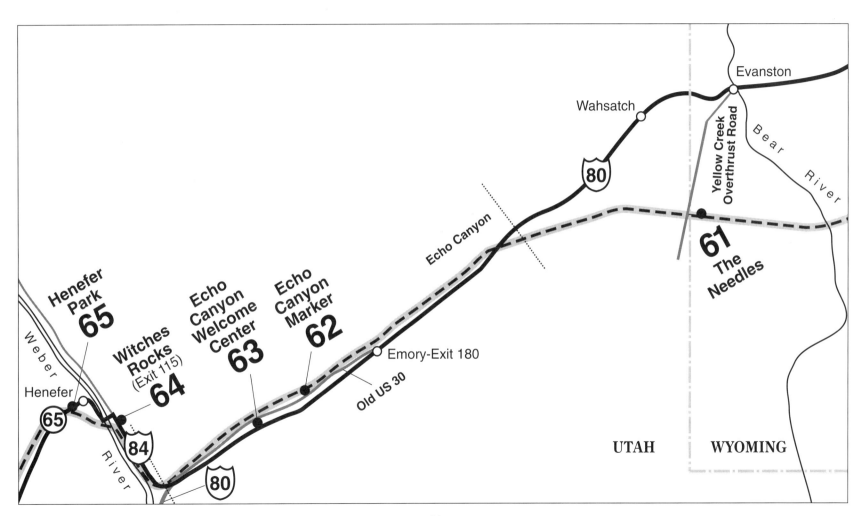

Henefer
Park
65

Witches
Rocks
(Exit 115)
64

Echo
Canyon
Welcome
Center
63

Echo
Canyon
Marker
62

Echo Canyon

Yellow Creek
Overthrust Road

61
The
Needles

Henefer

Weber

River

Emory-Exit 180

Old US 30

Wahsatch

Evanston

Bear River

UTAH

WYOMING

65

84

80

80

Mormon Pioneer, and Pony Express National Historic Trails, is located in a city park southwest of town on UT 65, which is designated the Pioneer Memorial Backway.

66. Spring Creek Station/Marker: About 3 miles up UT 65, southwest of Henefer, is located the Spring Creek Station historic site. This was a Mormon supply station during the "Utah War" of 1857-58.

67. Hogsback Summit Historic Site/Ruts: This site, sometimes called Heartbreak Ridge, is 6 miles southwest of Henefer, on UT 65. Here Mormons got their best (and disheartening) sight of the mountains they still had to pass through to reach their new Zion. About 100 yards back towards Henefer, just to the west of the road, may be seen about an eighth of a mile of rather poor trail ruts, some of the very few ruts left of the trail in Utah. A new wayside exhibit has replaced the old, vandalized marker.

Along UT 65, before and after the Hogsback Summit, are several other trail markers. Watch for them.

68. East Canyon State Park/Marker: Several miles southwest of Hogsback Summit is East Canyon State Park. A wayside exhibit is located near the boat ramp.

69. Large Spring Camp Historic Site/Marker: This site, an important campsite on the Mormon Pioneer Trail, is located a half mile north of the mouth of Little Emigration Canyon on a dirt road (See site 70).

70. Little Emigration Canyon Historic Site/Marker: Approximately 8 miles southwest of the Hogsback Summit, on UT 65, a dirt road goes left (south) for 3 miles to Mormon Flat, near the mouth of Little Emigration Canyon. A wayside exhibit and some stone breastworks from the Mormon War of 1857-58 can be seen here.

The old trail goes 4.3 miles up this gentle canyon and is the longest sustained climb anywhere on the trail. It is a pleasant hike to the crest of Big Mountain. (It is even more pleasant hiking down!)

71. Big Mountain Historic Site/Marker: This site is 19 miles southwest of Henefer, on UT 65, and is the place where the Pioneers of 1847 and thousands of subsequent emigrants caught their first view of their new home—the Valley of the Great Salt Lake.

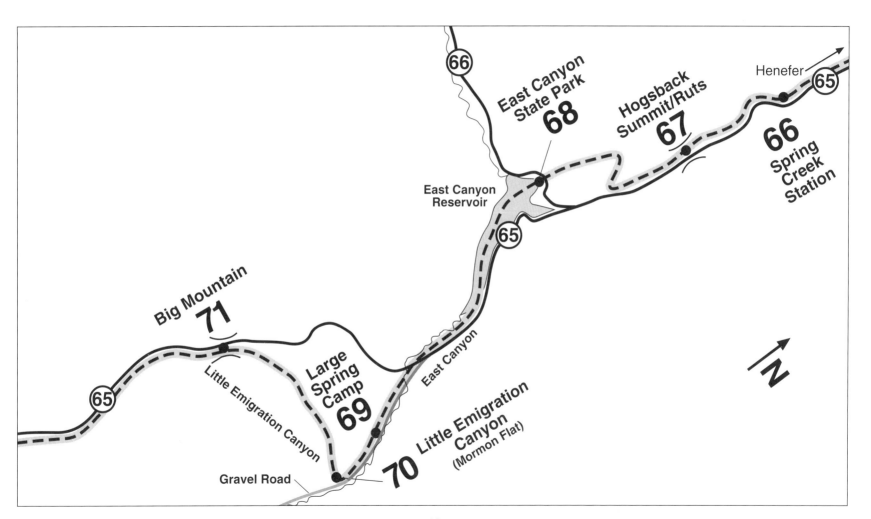

66
Spring
Creek
Station

Hogsback
Summit/Ruts
67

East Canyon
State Park
68

Henefer

66

65

East Canyon
Reservoir

65

Big Mountain
71

Large
Spring
Camp
69

Little Emigration Canyon

65

East Canyon

Little Emigration
Canyon
(Mormon Flat)
70

Gravel Road

N

72. Quaking Asp Grove/Marker: About 2 miles down Big Mountain is an old camp site where a new wayside exhibit has been erected.

73. Little Mountain/Marker: About 7 miles southwest of Big Mountain, on UT 65, the trail went up over Little Mountain and entered Emigration Canyon, the canyon that led directly, and finally, into the Valley of the Great Salt Lake.

To drive over Little Mountain into Emigration Canyon, take Emigration Canyon Road off UT 65, 5.9 miles from the crest of Big Mountain. Follow the signs to Emigration Canyon and the Pioneer Memorial Scenic Backway. Look for a marker at the crest of Little Mountain, 1.5 miles from the turnoff.

74. Last Camp Historic Site/Marker: About 2.6 miles below Little Mountain Summit, to the right of the road (just before Cromptons Restaurant) is the Last Camp historic marker.

75. Donner Hill Historic Site/Marker: About 4.5 miles down Emigration Canyon Road from the Last Camp marker is Donner Hill. The Donner-Reed party, worn out from moving boulders and cutting down dense undergrowth, unwisely left the canyon floor here and forced their animals over this hill.

This jaded their oxen and contributed to their eventual tragedy in the Sierra Nevadas.

76. This is the Place Monument: On Sunnyside Avenue (a continuation of Emigration Canyon Road), in This is the Place State Park, Salt Lake City. The monument was built in 1947 to commemorate the centennial of the arrival of the Pioneers into the Valley of the Great Salt Lake. This massive memorial, 60 feet high and 84 feet wide, was designed by Mahroni M. Young, Brigham's grandson. It features 15 plaques and many statues and bas-reliefs, which honor not only the Mormon Pioneers, but American Indians, and explorers of the Great Basin.

There is also a visitor center and the Old Deseret Village, an outdoor museum, in this 500-acre park, which commemorates the end of the famous Mormon Pioneer Trail from Nauvoo, Illinois, to Salt Lake City, Utah.

Also related to the Mormon Pioneer Trail in Salt Lake City are the museum of the Daughters of the Utah Pioneers and the Museum of Church History and Art of the Church of Jesus Christ of Latter-day Saints.

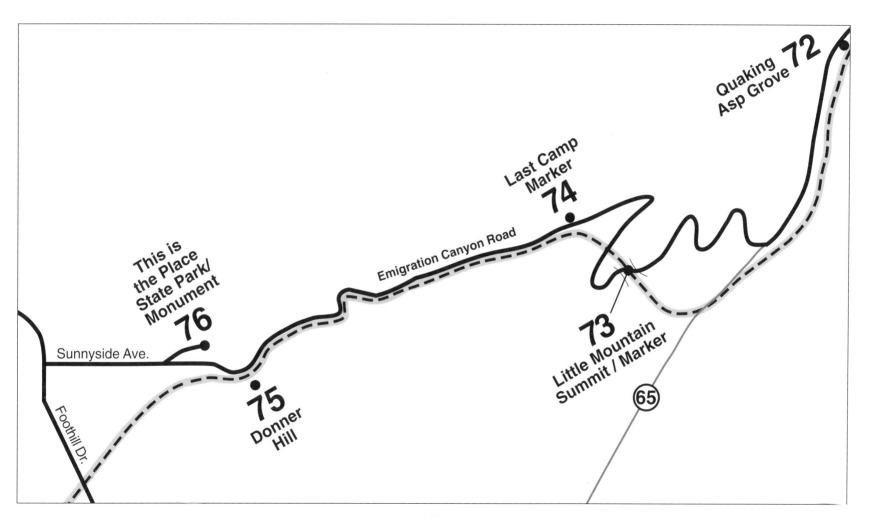

Quaking Asp Grove **72**

Last Camp Marker **74**

This is the Place State Park/ Monument **76**

Sunnyside Ave.

Foothill Dr.

Emigration Canyon Road

75 Donner Hill

73 Little Mountain Summit / Marker

(65)

Lynn Fausett – *Descent down Big Mountain*

For further information travelers are advised to refer to the Mormon Pioneer Trail brochure in the back of this publication, or write to the National Park Service, P.O. Box 45155, Salt Lake City, UT 84145-0155, and the Bureau of Land Management, P.O. Box 887, Casper, Wyoming 82602. Travelers may also wish to consult two trail guides prepared

by this author, *Historic Sites and Markers Along the Mormon and Other Great Western Trails.* Urbana: University of Illinois Press, 1988, and *Historic Resource Study: Mormon Pioneer National Historic Trail.* National Park Service, 1991. Trail literature is also available at visitor centers, museums, and tourist attractions along the trail.

Valoy Eaton – *Entering the Valley*